Eggless Desserts

100% Gelatine Free

~ Tarla Dalal ~
NO.1 BEST SELLING COOKERY AUTHOR

S&C

SANJAY & CO.,
MUMBAI.

Seventh Printing : 2006

Copyright© Sanjay & Co.

ISBN : 81-86469-19-2

Price Rs. 230/-

Published & Distributed by : **Sanjay & Company**
353/A-1, Shah & Nahar Industrial Estate, Dhanraj Mill Compound,
Lower Parel (W), Mumbai - 400 013. INDIA.
Tel. : (91-22) 2496 8068 Fax : (91-22) 2496 5876 E-mail : sanjay@tarladalal.com
Printed by : **Minal Sales Agencies**, Mumbai

: Design Concepts & Layouts : : Food Stylist : : Photography :
CountDown Advertising Leena Tandon Rajeev Asgaonkar

: Research Team : : Production Designers :
Pinky Chandan Lorella Jacinto
Prasad Lale

OTHER BOOKS BY TARLA DALAL

INDIAN COOKING
Tava Cooking
Rotis & Subzis
Desi Khana
The Complete Gujarati Cook Book
Mithai
Chaat
Achaar aur Parathe
The Rajasthani Cookbook
Swadisht Subzian

WESTERN COOKING
The Complete Italian Cookbook
The Chocolate Cookbook
Mocktails & Snacks
Soups & Salads
Mexican Cooking
Easy Gourmet Cooking
Chinese Cooking
Easy Chinese Cooking
Thai Cooking
Sizzlers & Barbeques

MINI SERIES
Idlis & Dosas
Cooking under 10 minutes
Pizzas and Pasta
Fun Food for Children
Roz Ka Khana
Microwave - Desi Khana
T.V. Meals
Paneer
Parathas
Chawal
Dals

Sandwiches
Quick Cooking
Curries & Kadhis
Chinese Recipes
Jain Desi Khana
7 Dinner Menus
Jain International Recipes
Punjabi Subzis
Corn
Microwave Subzis New

TOTAL HEALTH
Low Calorie Healthy Cooking
Pregnancy Cookbook
Baby and Toddler Cookbook
Cooking with 1 Teaspoon of Oil
Home Remedies
Delicious Diabetic Recipes
Fast Foods Made Healthy
Healthy Soups & Salads
Healthy Breakfast
Calcium Rich Recipes
Healthy Heart Cook Book
Forever Young Diet

Healthy Snacks
Iron Rich Recipes
Healthy Juices
Low Cholesterol Recipes
Good Food for Diabetes
Healthy Subzis
Healthy Snacks for Kids
High Blood Pressure Cook Book
Low Calorie Sweets New
Nutritious Recipes for Pregnancy New

GENERAL COOKING
Exciting Vegetarian Cooking
Microwave Recipes
Quick & Easy Cooking
Saatvik Khana
Mixer Cook Book
The Pleasures of Vegetarian Cooking
The Delights of Vegetarian Cooking
The Joys of Vegetarian Cooking
Cooking with Kids
Snacks Under 10 Minutes
Ice-Cream & Frozen Desserts
Desserts Under 10 Minutes
Entertaining
Microwave Snacks & Desserts

Introduction

No meal is complete without a dessert. An elegant dessert rounds off the success of a dinner party. Whether it's a special family dinner, a birthday, a festive occasion, or just to pamper your loved ones.

Today, buying a dessert is expensive and to get a vegetarian dessert is almost impossible. Keeping that in mind, here is a book which gives you a wide selection of mouthwatering desserts which are not only eggless but also gelatine free. Every recipe is researched and tested in our kitchen to ensure that you will have no difficulty in making them.

You will find that the preparation and cooking of the recipes are organised in easy-to-follow steps. It is vital to stick to the recommended ingredients, quantities and methods for basics such as cakes, doughs and batters so that you get the best results. Indeed, in sharing with you my favourite recipes and their techniques, you will not only learn to conjure up an exotic dessert but also gain a great deal of experience on how ingredients behave under given conditions. Also look for handy tips or short-cuts in little handfuls of information that will remain with you for a lifetime.

You will find within this book recipes for every occasion in a collection ranging from the simple to the elaborate and the sensational. Quick desserts, cakes, tarts, pies and crepes with a special section on Indian desserts which are innovative and simple to follow.

Some of these desserts will satisfy your artistic talents while others are just right for busy mums with families to feed. Have fun with these recipes! Doing something new can be both creative and rewarding and you will be proud to present these delicacies as if they were your own creations.

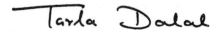

3

INDEX

Glossary

Double boiler

Double boiler is a pot of boiling or simmering hot water over which you place a smaller pot containing the ingredient you want to heat. eg. chocolate.

Fold

Combine ingredients lightly to prevent loss of air. Using a spatula or wooden spoon, cut down into the centre of the bowl, vertically. Then scoop under the contents in a circular motion and them cut vertically again. Repeat this until the ingredients are uniformly combined.

Cut in / Rub in

To distribute solid fat into dry ingredients until you get a coarse grainy texture.
eg. : butter and flour in a tart recipe.

Beat

Combine ingredients thoroughly by mixing vigorously to make a mixture smooth and free of lumps.

Creaming

To beat fat with a wooden spoon till it is light and fluffy.

Grease and flour

Rub the inside surface of a baking tin with butter or margarine and then dust lightly with flour to prevent the food from sticking while baking. After dusting the baking tin with flour, turn it upside down and tap the bottom to remove excess flour.

Glaze

To coat a food with jelly or syrup to add lustre or shine to the food.
eg. : coating a fruit with a warm syrup to keep it from discolouring and for maintaining a gloss.

Core

To remove the centre of a fruit (apple, pear, pineapple). This can be done using a knife or a corer, usually attached to a peeler.

Hull

To remove the leaves by cutting off a little from the top of a fruit. eg. : strawberries.

Measuring Spoons

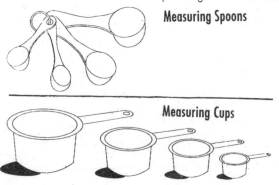

Measuring Cups

Loose Bottomed Tin

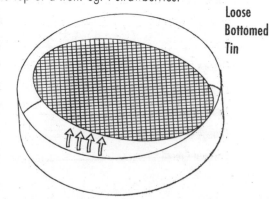

Indian Desserts

The best representation of India's colourful diversity is to be found in its culinary heritage, wherein besides food, traditional Indian mithais have carved a niche all their very own. 'Petha' from Delhi, the humble 'Rossogolla' from Calcutta, the Mathura 'Pedha' or Mysore 'Pak' are always important items on any traveller's shopping list.

Yet as time moves on and tastes change, the demand for variety is ever growing. In this section, you will find just that; part tradition and part culinary innovation blended into successfully tested combinations and colourful presentations to impress both family and guests.

Firni

A traditional rice custard cooked with milk and set in earthenware containers.

Preparation time : 40 minutes	Cooking time : 20 minutes	Serves 6 to 8

1 litre milk (full cream)
4 tablespoons Basmati rice
6 tablespoons sugar
½ teaspoon cardamom powder

For the garnish

a few chopped almonds

1. Soak the rice in water for about 1 hour.
2. Drain all the water and powder the rice in a mixer.
3. Add half a cup of cold milk to the rice powder and make a paste.
4. Boil the rest of the milk and gently stir in the rice paste.
5. Cook for about 15 minutes on a slow flame, stirring continuously.
6. Add the sugar and cardamom powder and simmer for a few minutes.

Cool and serve in earthenware containers.
Garnish with chopped almonds.

Handy Tip

~ Milk thickens quicker in a broad bottomed non-stick pan. Use one for best results and to save time.

Variation

~ KESARI FIRNI : Add a little saffron to the sugar and cardamom powder and proceed as per the recipe.

Carrot Pancakes With Rabdi

A unique East - West blending of desserts. Carrot Halwa, a sweetmeat popular all over India, rolled within freshly made pancakes, topped with thickened milk and baked in a casserole.

Preparation time : 20 minutes	Cooking time : 40 minutes	Makes 12 pancakes

For the pancakes, page 74

For the carrot halwa

4 teacups grated carrots

8 tablespoons sugar

5 tablespoons milk powder

2 teaspoons almonds, sliced

a pinch cardamom powder

2 tablespoons ghee

For the rabdi, page 102

For the garnish

50 grams sliced almonds

For the carrot halwa

1. Steam the grated carrots over boiling water for 3 minutes.
2. Heat the ghee, add the steamed carrots and sauté for 2 minutes.
3. Add the sugar and cook for 2 to 3 minutes. Then add the milk powder and cook for a few minutes, stirring continuously.
4. Add the almonds and sprinkle the cardamom powder on top.

How to proceed

1. Spread a little halwa on each pancake and roll up.
2. Arrange the pancakes on a baking dish, spread a little rabdi on top of each pancake and bake in a hot oven at 200ºC (400°F) for 5 to 10 minutes.

Serve hot, garnished with chopped almonds.

Handy Tips

~ You could safely prepare the pancakes a day in advance and refrigerate them. You could also prepare the carrot halwa and rabdi in advance.

~ When you wish to serve the pancakes, dip the box of refrigerated pancakes in hot water for at least two minutes.

~ A small quantity of rabdi can be made very quickly in a broad non-stick vessel.

Apple Jalebi

Hot batter-fried crispy apple rings coated in a fragrant saffron syrup.

Preparation time : 15 minutes	Cooking time : 20 minutes	Makes 12 jalebis

12 apple rings

1 cup plain flour (maida)

¼ teaspoon dry yeast

1 tablespoon melted ghee

1 teaspoon sugar

oil for deep frying

For the sugar syrup

1 cup sugar

½ teaspoon saffron

2 teaspoons rose water

For the garnish

½ teaspoon cardamom powder

1 tablespoon blanched & sliced pistachios

rose petals (optional)

1. Add the yeast and 2 pinches of sugar to ½ cup of lukewarm water. Mix well.

2. Sprinkle 2 pinches of flour on top. Cover and keep for 3 to 4 minutes. If the cup is full of froth, the yeast is ready to use.

3. Mix the flour, sugar, melted ghee and yeast liquid and some warm water until the mixture has the consistency of a thick batter.

4. Cover and keep for 40 to 50 minutes. Mix well again.

5. Dip the apple rings in this batter and deep fry in oil both sides until crisp. Drain.

For the sugar syrup

1. Dissolve the sugar in 1 cup of water and boil for 5 minutes.

2. Warm the saffron in a small vessel, add a little milk and rub until the saffron dissolves. Add to the syrup.

Handy Tip

~ As this batter is a little difficult to handle, make sure it coats the apple rings evenly. Persevere and the results will be worth the trouble.

10

3. Add the rose water.

4. Keep the syrup warm. The syrup should be of 1 thread consistency.

How to proceed

1. Remove the hot syrup from the flame and drop the fried apple rings into it. Soak for 1 minute and drain.

2. Sprinkle with the cardamom powder, pistachios and rose petals.

Serve hot.

Tava Chenna Peach Delight

A selection of juicy fruits encased between 2 layers of lightly fried paneer.

Preparation time : 10 minutes	Cooking time : 10 minutes	Serves 4

200 grams paneer, grated, page 108

1 tablespoon plain flour (maida)

4 tablespoons powdered sugar

some chopped fruits (strawberries, canned peaches, canned pineapple)

ghee for cooking

For serving

orange sauce, page 103

1. Mix the paneer, sugar and flour and knead well.

2. Divide into 2 portions.

3. Press half the mixture into a 125 mm. (5") square or round dish.

4. Spread the fruit pieces on top.

5. Cover with the remaining mixture and press well.

6. Chill for ½ hour.

7. Cut into small squares.

8. Cook on a tava on both sides with a little ghee.

Serve hot with chilled orange sauce.

Handy Tip

~ Cook these on a gentle flame, so that they brown evenly and also so that the paneer does not stick or crumble.

Coconut Paneer Rolls In Apple Rabdi

Grated coconut and paneer, evenly blended into rolls and served with an apple flavoured rabdi.

Preparation time : 15 to 20 minutes   Cooking time : 15 minutes   Makes 20 balls

For the coconut paneer rolls

250 grams paneer, grated, page 108

6 tablespoons powdered sugar

1 to 2 teaspoons rose water

a few drops rose essence

1½ teacups grated fresh coconut

¾ teacup sugar

1 pinch saffron

a little milk

¼ teaspoon cardamom powder

For the apple rabdi

½ litre milk (full fat)

2 tablespoons sugar

1 dessert apple, peeled and grated

For the garnish

2 to 3 blanched and chopped pistachios

¼ tablespoon cardamom powder

2 almonds, blanched and sliced

For the coconut paneer rolls

1. Mix the paneer, powdered sugar, rose water and essence.

2. Cook the coconut and sugar for 10 minutes on a slow flame. Cool.

3. Warm the saffron in a small vessel. Add a little milk and rub in until the saffron dissolves.

4. Add the saffron liquid and cardamom powder to the coconut mixture. Mix well.

5. Mix the paneer and coconut mixture together. Divide into 20 portions and shape into small rolls.

For the apple rabdi

1. Put the milk in a broad vessel and boil.

2. Add the sugar and cook on a slow flame while stirring continuously, until the mixture is reduced to half.

3. Add the grated apples to the milk, give one boil and remove from the heat at once. Cool and keep aside.

How to proceed

1. Arrange the rolls on a serving dish.

2. Pour the rabdi over it.

3. Garnish with pistachios and sprinkle almonds and cardamom powder on top.

Serve chilled.

Stuffed Malpuas With Paneer And Strawberry In Saffron Syrup

An exciting combination of fried malpuas soaked in saffron syrup and stuffed with fresh strawberries, crumbled paneer and dried fruit.

Preparation time : 5 minutes	Cooking time : 20 minutes	Makes 12 malpuas

For the malpuas

200 grams fresh cream

4 tablespoons plain flour (maida)

ghee for frying

For the filling

4 tablespoons crumbled paneer, page 108

4 tablespoons chopped strawberries

1 tablespoon chopped almonds and raisins

2 tablespoons powdered sugar

1 teaspoon rose water

For the saffron syrup

1 teacup sugar

2 pinches saffron

2 teaspoons milk

2 teaspoons rose water (optional)

For the garnish

sliced strawberries

For the malpuas

1. Mix the cream and flour into a batter.

2. Smear very little ghee on a frying pan and spread a small amount of the batter on it.

3. Fry on both sides using a little ghee until golden brown.

4. Place the malpuas in the warm saffron syrup for 2 to 3 minutes and drain.

Handy Tips

~ If strawberries are not in season, you can use pineapple or mango.

~ You can also omit the filling and serve the malpuas with rabdi, page **102**.

For the filling

1. Mix the paneer, strawberries, almonds, raisins and powdered sugar.
2. Add the rose water and keep aside.

For the saffron syrup

1. Dissolve the sugar in 1 cup of water and simmer for 5 minutes to make a syrup of 1 thread consistency.
2. Warm the saffron in a small vessel, add the milk and rub until the saffron dissolves. Add to the syrup.
3. Add the rose water and keep the syrup warm.

How to proceed

Fill each malpua with a little filling and fold into half.

Serve garnished with strawberry slices.

Strawberry Rasmalai

A fruity presentation of fresh strawberries sandwiched between slices of juicy rasmalai

Preparation time : 10 minutes	No cooking	Makes 12 rasmalais

12 rasmalais
1 cup sliced strawberries
1 tablespoon powdered sugar

1. Sprinkle the powdered sugar over the sliced strawberries.
2. Slice the rasmalais and sandwich them with a few sliced strawberries.
3. Crush the remaining strawberries and add to the rasmalai milk.

Arrange on a serving dish and garnish with a few sliced strawberries.

Handy Tip

~ Slice the rasmalais carefully as they are delicate and could break easily.

Variation

~ MANGO RASMALAI :
Use mangoes instead of strawberries.

Sunrise Surprise

Stewed apple rings topped with freshly cooked rabdi and nuts. An immensely pleasing visual presentation.

Preparation time : 10 minutes	Cooking time : 25 minutes	Serves 6

12 apple rings, peeled and cored

For the sugar syrup

1 cup sugar

½ teaspoon saffron

2 teaspoons rose water or kewda essence

For the rabdi

1 cup rabdi, page 102

½ cup fresh bread crumbs

For the garnish

½ teaspoon cardamom powder

1 tablespoon blanched & sliced pistachios

rose petals (optional)

For the sugar syrup

1. Dissolve the sugar in 1 cup of water and boil for 2 or 3 minutes.
2. Warm the saffron in a small vessel, add a little water and rub until the saffron dissolves. Add to the syrup.
3. Flavour with the rose water or kewda essence.

For the rabdi

1. Proceed as per the basic recipe.
2. Add the fresh bread crumbs and thicken the rabdi.

Handy Tip

~ Use very firm apples as they tend to break while cooking. Handle them very gently using a slotted spoon.

Top to Bottom : Strawberry Soufflé, page 91;
Fruit Brochettes, page 83;
Fruit Sandesh, page 19.

➤

16

How to proceed

1. Cook the apple slices in the syrup for 1 minute, taking care to ensure they do not break.

2. Place the apple slices on a serving dish and pour half the syrup over it.

3. Spoon out some rabdi onto the centre of each apple ring.

4. Pour some syrup over the rabdi and garnish with chopped pistachios and cardamom powder.

Serve immediately.

Fruit Sandesh   Picture on page 17

Creamy sandesh (Bengali classic) topped with fresh fruits.

Preparation time : a few minutes	No cooking	Serves 4

2 cups freshly made paneer, page 108

4 to 6 tablespoons icing sugar

a few drops of kewda essence or rose water

1 cup fresh fruits

1. Knead the paneer with the sugar to form a smooth dough. Add the kewda essence and knead again.

2. Divide the mixture into 2 parts and slightly sauté 1 part in a non-stick pan for about 4 to 5 minutes.

3. Mix the sautéed dough with the remaining dough and knead again.

4. Roll out this mixture to 12.5 mm. (½") thickness.

5. Using a cookie cutter, cut out rounds and place on serving plates.

Decorate with sliced fruits of your choice.

Chill and serve.

Handy Tips

~ Best if freshly made. Try not to store for more than a day or two.

~ You can use a tablespoon of fresh cream to soften the paneer dough.

◄ Mango Cheesecake, page 44.

Cakes & Gateaux

Fruity, spongy, nutty or oozing with chocolate and cream!!! You don't really need an occasion to bake a cake and yet it becomes a celebration in itself. Whether bought or baked, a cake is always devoured with equal relish, and if any guest asked you where you bought it from, wouldn't you be proud to say "I baked it".

This Cakes & Gateaux section goes on to teach you eggless versions of popular international favourites plus my very own recipes, perfected over the years.

Eggless Sponge Cake

Preparation time : 10 minutes   **Baking time : 30 minutes**   **Serves 4 to 6**

½ can condensed milk (400 grams for full can)

140 grams self-raising flour

1 level teaspoon baking powder

½ teaspoon soda bi-carb

60 ml. melted butter or margarine

1 teaspoon vanilla essence

1. Sieve the flour, baking powder and soda bi-carb together.

2. Mix the flour mixture, condensed milk, melted butter, essence and 75 ml. of water and beat well.

3. Pour the mixture into a greased and dusted 150 mm. (6") diameter tin.

4. Bake in a hot oven at 200ºC (400°F) for 10 minutes. Then reduce the temperature to 150°C (300°F) and a bake for a further 15 minutes.

5. The cake is ready when it leaves the sides of the tin and is springy to touch. When ready, remove from the oven and leave for 1 minute. Invert the tin over a rack and tap sharply to remove.

6. Cool the cake.

Handy Tips

~ When greasing tins for cakes, use hydrogenated fat (vanaspati).

~ While filling the batter, fill cake tins only ¾ full to allow for rising.

~ Pre-heat the oven before using for 15 to 20 minutes.

Slicing a cake into two layers

Eggless Chocolate Sponge Cake

| Preparation time : 10 minutes | Baking time : 30 minutes | Serves 4 to 6 |

½ can (400 grams for full can) condensed milk

125 grams self-raising flour

2 tablespoons cocoa powder

1 level teaspoon baking powder

½ teaspoon soda bi-carb

60 ml. melted butter or margarine

1 teaspoon vanilla essence

1. Sieve the flour, cocoa powder, baking powder and soda bi-carb together.

2. Mix the condensed milk, flour mixture, 100 ml. of water, the vanilla essence and melted butter thoroughly.

3. Pour the cake mixture into a greased and dusted 150 mm. or 175 mm. (6" or 7") diameter tin.

4. Bake in a hot oven at 200ºC (400ºF) for 10 minutes. Then reduce the temperature to 180ºC (350ºF) and bake for a further 15 minutes.

5. The cake is ready when it leaves the sides of the tin and is springy to touch. When ready, takeout from the oven and leave for 1 minute. Invert the tin over a rack and tap sharply to remove.

6. Cool the cake.

Handy Tips

~ To test if the cake is done, pierce a wooden tooth-pick through it. If it comes out clean the cake is done.

~ Bake the cake in the middle of the oven as this corresponds most exactly with the dial setting.

~ Always let the cake cool slightly before removing from tin.

Slicing a cake into two layers

Baba Surprise

A ring of delicate sponge cake, soaked in a syrup flavoured with lemon juice and rum and filled with ice-cream and nuts.

Preparation time : 20 minutes	Baking time : 35 minutes	Serves 4 to 6

For the sponge cake ring

1 recipe eggless sponge cake, page 22

To be mixed into a soaking syrup

100 grams sugar

juice of 1 lemon

1½ cups water

1 teaspoon rum (optional)

For the filling

2 tablespoons mixed dried fruit

2 scoops vanilla ice-cream

For the decoration

1 cup whipped cream, page 106

a few cherries

For the sponge cake ring

1. Follow the basic recipe, except use a ring mould of 160 mm. (6½") diameter and bake in a preheated oven at 180ºC (350ºF) for 35 minutes.

2. Turn out and allow to cool.

How to proceed

1. Place the sponge ring on a serving dish.

2. Saturate it with the soaking syrup.

3. Pipe the whipped cream around the base.

4. Just before serving, fill the centre with the ice-cream. Sprinkle dried fruits on top.

Garnish with cherries.

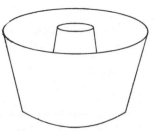

Ring Mould

Strawberry Hearts

A freshly baked heart shaped sponge cake soaked and sandwiched with whipped cream and strawberries and garnished with sliced strawberries.

Preparation time : 20 minutes	Baking time : 25 minutes	Serves 4 to 6

For the sponge cake

1 recipe eggless sponge cake, page 22

For the filling

1 cup whipped cream, page 106

1 cup sliced strawberries

1 tablespoon powdered sugar

To be mixed into a soaking syrup

1 teacup water

3 teaspoons powdered sugar

1 tablespoon brandy (optional)

2 tablespoons strawberry juice

For the garnish

1 cup whipped cream, page 106

6 whole strawberries

For the sponge cake

1. Follow the basic recipe except use a heart-shaped cake tin and bake in a hot oven at 200ºC (400ºF) for 25 minutes.

2. Cool and slice into 2 parts horizontally.

For the filling

1. Mash the strawberries lightly. Add the powdered sugar and keep aside for ½ hour.

2. Mix the strawberries with the whipped cream.

Handy Tip

~ If you do not have a heart shaped mould, use a round tin and then when the sponge is cool, cut out a heart shape by using a paper cutting placed on the cake.

Variation

~ Chocolate lovers can use a chocolate sponge instead of a plain sponge.

How to proceed

1. Soak the sponge with the soaking syrup.

2. Spread the filling mixture over one part of the cake.

3. Put the other part of the cake on top.

4. Pipe the border of the cake with a little cream.

5. Fill the centre with strawberries.

6. Refrigerate the cake.

When you want to serve, cut into slices and serve cold.

Tiramisu

An elegant and exotic Italian dessert of sponge cake soaked with coffee and Kahlua and sandwiched with fresh custard cream.

Preparation time : 20 minutes | **Baking time : 30 minutes** | **Serves 4 to 6**

1 eggless sponge cake, page 22

To be mixed into a soaking syrup

1 cup black coffee

1/3 cup Kahlua (optional)

For the custard cream

1½ cups milk

5 to 6 teaspoons sugar

4 teaspoons custard powder

½ teaspoon vanilla essence

3 tablespoons thick cream

sherry or rum to taste (optional)

For the garnish

1 tablespoon coffee powder

For the custard cream

1. Mix the custard powder with a little milk.
2. Put the balance milk with the sugar to boil.
3. When the milk starts boiling, add the custard powder mixture and cook for 1 minute. Cool.
4. Add the cream, vanilla essence and sherry and mix well.

How to proceed

1. Divide the cake into 2 parts. Soak thoroughly with the soaking syrup.
2. Place one layer of the cake on a serving dish. Spread half of the custard cream over it.
3. Cover with the other layer of cake. Spread the balance custard cream.
4. Sprinkle coffee powder on top to decorate.

Serve chilled.

Handy Tip

~You can use rum instead of Kahlua.

Ile Flottante (Floating Islands)

*Small islands of vanilla sponge sandwiched with whipped cream &
strawberries floating in a strawberry sauce.*

Preparation time : **20 minutes**	Baking time : **30 minutes**	Serves **3**

For the cake

1 round eggless sponge cake, page 22

To be mixed into a soaking syrup

2 tablespoons sugar

2 tablespoons strawberry juice

½ cup water

For the filling

1 cup whipped cream, page 106

1 cup sliced strawberries

1 tablespoon powdered sugar

For the sauce

1 cup fresh strawberries

¼ cup sugar

2 tablespoons lemon juice

For the garnish

3 strawberries

For the filling

1. Sprinkle the powdered sugar over the sliced strawberries and keep aside.

2. Keep the cream refrigerated until ready to use.

For the sauce

1. Extract juice from the strawberries by rubbing through a fine strainer or purée
the fruit in an electric blender.

2. Add the sugar and lemon juice and mix very well.

Cookie Cutter

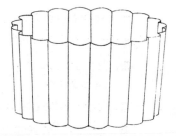

How to proceed

1. Using a 75 mm. (3") diameter cookie cutter, cut three rounds from the sponge cake.

2. Slice each horizontally. Sprinkle with the soaking syrup.

3. Fill with the strawberries and whipped cream and top with the other half of the sponge.

4. Sprinkle the top layer with the soaking syrup and garnish with one whole strawberry.

How to serve

Place all three small cakes on a serving dish and pour the strawberry sauce all around to resemble floating islands.

Refrigerate before serving.

Pineapple Upside Down

A well known American speciality of pineapple baked along with sponge cake and served with whipped cream.

Preparation time : 20 minutes	Baking time : 1 hour	Serves 6 to 8

For the batter

140 grams plain flour (maida)

1 teaspoon baking powder

½ teaspoon soda bicarbonate

60 ml. melted butter

½ cup sugar

½ can condensed milk (full can is 400 grams)

3 tablespoons milk

For the fruit arrangement

1 fresh pineapple, peeled, cored & cut into rings

2 tablespoons golden syrup

10 glazed cherries

1 tablespoon butter

For the batter

1. Mix the flour, baking powder, soda bicarbonate, melted butter, sugar and condensed milk and beat well.

2. Add enough milk to give the batter a dropping consistency.

For the fruit arrangement

1. Grease a 200 mm. (8") **diameter** cake tin with a little butter.

2. Spread the golden syrup evenly on the base of the tin. Arrange the pineapple slices decoratively on the top of the golden syrup and place a glazed cherry in the centre of each ring.

How to proceed

1. Preheat the oven to 180°C (350°F).

2. Pour the batter carefully into the cake tin and smooth down the top of the

Handy Tips

~ If you do not have golden syrup, use brown sugar creamed in butter.

~ Use a little pineapple syrup to flavour the cake batter.

30

batter.

3. Bake in the oven for 50 minutes to 1 hour until the cake is golden brown.

4. Remove and allow to cool.

5. Run a knife around the sides and invert on a serving dish.

Cut into small portions and serve.

Strawberry Sponge Roll

Picture on page 72

A Swiss Roll presentation with strawberries and custard rolled within thin lightened sponge cake.

| Preparation time: 20 minutes | Baking time: 20 minutes | Cooking time: 10 minutes | Serves 4 to 6 |

For the sponge roll

¼ can condensed milk (full can is 400 grams)

70 grams plain flour (maida)

½ teaspoon baking powder

a pinch soda bi carbonate

30 ml. melted butter or margarine

½ teaspoon vanilla essence

rind of 1 large orange or 1 teaspoon marmalade

To be mixed into a soaking syrup

¾ cup water

3 tablespoons powdered sugar

To be mixed into a strawberry filling

½ cup fresh strawberries, washed, hulled and chopped coarsely

6 tablespoons powdered sugar

For the custard

1 cup milk

2 tablespoons custard powder

1 tablespoon sugar

For the garnish

¼ cup fresh strawberries

2 tablespoons castor sugar

For the sponge roll

1. Preheat the oven to 200°C (400°F).

2. Line a 200 mm. x 300 mm. (8" x 12") Swiss roll tin with grease-proof or

Handy Tip

~ The baked sponge should be rolled while still warm as otherwise it could harden or crack and become difficult to roll.

waxed paper and set aside.

3. In a bowl, mix the ingredients with the orange rind and 30 ml. of water and beat well.

4. Spoon the mixture into the prepared Swiss roll tin and smoothen the edges.

5. Bake in the preheated oven for 15 to 20 minutes until the sponge is golden brown and springs back when lightly pressed with the fingertips.

For the custard

1. Dissolve the custard powder in a little cold milk.

2. Boil the rest of the milk with the sugar.

3. Add the custard powder and simmer for a few minutes.

4. Cool and keep aside in the refrigerator.

How to proceed

1. Soak the sponge lightly with the refrigerated soaking syrup.

2. Spread the cold custard on the sponge.

3. Spoon the strawberry filling evenly over the custard.

4. Carefully lift one end of the greaseproof paper and roll up the sponge.

5. Transfer to a serving dish. Arrange the whole strawberries over and around the roll. Sprinkle the castor sugar over it.

Serve chilled.

Gateau Mount Pleasant

Chocolate Sponge sandwiched with rum flavoured apple purée and topped with walnut praline and apple rings.

Preparation time: 20 minutes	Baking time: 30 minutes	Cooking time: 5 to 10 minutes	Serves 4 to 6

For the sponge cake

1 eggless chocolate sponge cake, page 23

For the filling

4 to 5 dessert apples, peeled, cored and sliced

½ teaspoon ground cinnamon

4 tablespoons sugar

2 tablespoons rum (optional)

To be mixed into a soaking syrup

2 tablespoons sugar

1 cup water

For the topping

8 tablespoons walnut praline, page 102

1½ cups whipped cream, page 106

For the filling

1. Cook the apples in a saucepan with the cinnamon, sugar and 2 tablespoons of water to form a thick purée. Cool.

2. Add the rum.

How to proceed

1. Slice the sponge cake horizontally into two layers.

2. Soak the layers with the soaking syrup.

3. Sandwich together both the layers of the cake with the apple purée.

4. Spread the whipped cream evenly on the top and sides.

5. Sprinkle the crushed praline over it.

Gateau Mount Pleasant, above.

Handy Tips

~ Always use a stainless steel blade to cut apples and bananas as iron blades blacken the fruit.

~ Sprinkle a little lemon juice on the apple slices to prevent discoloration.

Variation

~ COFFEE APPLE GATEAU : You can add coffee powder to the whipped cream. (Picture on facing page 35)

➤

Mocha Brandy Cake

A sponge cake glazed with a generous helping of coffee, cocoa and brandy, topped with whipped cream and almond flakes.

| Preparation time: 15 minutes | Baking time: 30 minutes | Cooking time: 10 minutes | Serves 4 to 6 |

For the sponge cake

I recipe eggless sponge cake, page 22
1 tablespoon coffee powder

For the glaze

100 grams granulated sugar
1 tablespoon strong black coffee
1 tablespoon cocoa powder
2 tablespoons brandy

For the decoration

1½ cups whipped cream, page 106
a few flaked almonds

For the sponge cake

Proceed as mentioned in the basic recipe, adding the coffee powder to the batter.

For the glaze

1. Put the sugar, black coffee, cocoa powder and 4 tablespoons of water in a saucepan and stir until the solids are dissolved.
2. Bring to the boil on a low flame and simmer for 5 minutes.
3. Remove from the heat and add the brandy.

How to proceed

1. Prick the cake all over with a fork.
2. Pour the glaze over the cake and leave to soak.

Decorate with the whipped cream and almond flakes.

◄ Ebony & Ivory, page 40.

Tropical Cake

A sumptuous dessert of sponge soaked in brandy and orange juice sandwiched with banana, whipped cream and walnuts.

Preparation time : 20 minutes   **Baking time : 30 minutes**   **Serves 4 to 6**

For the sponge cake

1 recipe eggless sponge cake, page 22

grated rind of 1 lemon

For the banana filling

3 ripe bananas

juice of 3 oranges

¾ cup walnuts, chopped

To be mixed into a soaking syrup

juice of 1½ oranges

¼ cup brandy

2 tablespoons sugar

¾ cup walnuts, chopped

For the garnish

2 cups whipped cream, page 106

¾ cup walnuts, halved

sliced bananas

For the sponge cake

1. Prepare the sponge as directed adding the lemon rind to the batter.

2. Bake as specified and cool.

3. Slice horizontally into two.

For the banana filling

1. Peel and slice the bananas.

2. Place the sliced bananas in the soaking syrup.

Handy Tips

~ You can use orange liqueur instead of brandy.

~ Slice bananas to garnish the dessert just before serving so they do not blacken.

3. Keep the walnuts aside.

How to proceed

1. Drain the bananas from the syrup and soak the bottom layer of the sponge cake with the soaking syrup.

2. Spread half the whipped cream on the soaked layer of sponge.

3. Place all the drained bananas on top and sprinkle chopped walnuts on them.

4. Top with the second layer of sponge cake and then soak with the soaking syrup.

5. Spread another layer of the remaining whipped cream evenly.

Garnish with sliced bananas and halved walnuts.

Ebony And Ivory   Picture on page 36

A delicious chocolate sponge, in a bittersweet fantasy of chocolate cake sandwiched with pineapple, coconut and white chocolate mousse, topped with a chocolate glaze.

Preparation time: 20 minutes	Baking time: 30 minutes	Setting time: 1 hour	Serves 4 to 6

For the sponge cake
1 eggless chocolate sponge cake, page 23

To be mixed into a soaking syrup
2 tablespoons powdered sugar
1 cup water

For the white chocolate filling
1 cup white chocolate, grated
1 cup whipped cream, page 106
2 pineapple slices, finely chopped
2 tablespoons desiccated coconut

For the dark chocolate topping
½ cup dark chocolate, grated
½ cup whipped cream, page 106

For the garnish
flaked almonds
orange segments
whipped cream, page 106

For the white chocolate filling
1. Melt the grated white chocolate over a double boiler till it is a smooth paste. Cool slightly.
2. Fold in the whipped cream gently along with chopped pineapple and desiccated coconut.
3. Keep aside.

Grease Proof Paper

For the dark chocolate topping

1. Melt the grated dark chocolate over a double boiler. Cool slightly.

2. Fold in the whipped cream. Keep aside.

3. Make the topping once the cake has been sandwiched and refrigerated.

How to proceed

1. Slice the sponge cake horizontally into 2 slices.

2. Place the lower half on a serving dish and generously soak with the refrigerated soaking syrup.

3. Spread the white chocolate filling mixture evenly on this layer. Use a 75 mm. (3") strip of greaseproof paper to line the sides of the cake, so that the filling does not spill over (refer to diagram on page 40).

4. Top with the other layer of sponge and soak it well with the refrigerated soaking syrup.

5. Refrigerate for at least 1 hour, till the filling mixture has set.

6. Remove the greaseproof paper, then top with a thin layer of the dark chocolate topping.

Decorate the sides with almond flakes.

On the top, pipe swirls whipped cream and orange segments.

Rich Chocolate Mousse Cake

A lightly soaked chocolate sponge topped with a layer of chocolate mousse and garnished with freshly whipped cream and grated chocolate.

Preparation time : 15 minutes   Baking time : 30 minutes   Serves 6 to 8
Cooking time : 15 minutes   Setting time : 1 hour

For the chocolate sponge cake

1 eggless chocolate sponge cake, page 23, sliced horizontally into two

For the chocolate mousse

1¼ cups milk

5 teaspoons cocoa powder

50 grams dark chocolate, grated

5 grams agar agar (China grass)

1 teaspoon custard powder

100 grams whipped cream, page 106

½ teaspoon vanilla essence

1 tablespoon sugar

To be mixed into a soaking syrup

½ cup water

1 tablespoon sugar

For the garnish

1 cup whipped cream, page 106
grated chocolate

For the chocolate sponge cake

1. Use only one layer of the sponge.

2. Use the other layer for the 'VARIATION'.

For the chocolate mousse

1. Soak the agar agar in ¾ cup of cold water for 1 hour. Heat on a slow flame until it dissolves.

Handy Tip

~ If you like, add a dash of rum to the soaking syrup.

Variation

~ With the remaining layer of sponge, make a CHOCOLATE SUNDAE GATEAU by soaking it with the soaking syrup, and topping it with scoops of vanilla ice-cream. Serve accompanied by Fudge Sauce, page 104.

2. Put 1 cup of milk to boil with the sugar, cocoa powder and dark chocolate.

3. To the balance ¼ cup milk, add the custard powder and boil. When the milk starts boiling, add to the cocoa mixture and go on stirring and cooking for 1 minute.

4. When the agar agar is dissolved completely, add to the boiling custard and cook again for 2 minutes.

5. Strain the mixture and go on stirring until it is slightly cool.

6. Gently fold in the whipped cream into the cocoa mix, add the vanilla essence and mix well.

How to proceed

1. Place one layer of the chocolate sponge on a 200 mm. (8") diameter loose bottom cake tin.

2. Sprinkle the soaking syrup on the cake and pour the mousse mixture on top.

3. Refrigerate till set.

4. When you wish to serve, unmould from the tin and serve garnished with whipped cream and grated chocolate.

Mango Cheesecake   Picture on page 18

A soft vanilla sponge cake with a topping of creamy mango cheesecake, garnished with finely sliced mango.

Preparation time : 15 minutes	Baking time : 30 minutes	Setting time : 1 hour	Serves 4 to 6

For the sponge cake

1 eggless sponge cake, page 22

For the cheesecake mixture

1 recipe cream cheese, page 108
2 mangoes, peeled and cut into pieces
4 tablespoons thick curds
½ cup cream
¾ cup castor sugar

To be mixed into a soaking syrup

1 cup water
1 tablespoon sugar

For the garnish

a few mango slices

For the sponge cake

1. Slice the sponge cake into two horizontally. Use only one layer of the sponge.
2. Use the other layer for the variation.

For the cheesecake mix

1. Liquidize the cream cheese, mango pieces, curds and sugar to a smooth purée in a blender.
2. Whip the cream till soft peaks form and mix gently with the mango mixture.

How to proceed

1. Place one layer of the sponge cake on the bottom of a loose bottomed 150 mm. (6") diameter cake tin.
2. Sprinkle the soaking syrup over the sponge.
3. Pour the cheesecake mixture over the sponge and refrigerate till set. Unmould from the tin.

Serve chilled garnished with mango slices.

Handy Tips

~ Hang curds in a muslin cloth for 10-15 minutes to get thick curds.

~ For a larger crowd, use the other slice of sponge cake and make another cheesecake.

Variation

~ With the remaining layer of sponge, make a MANGO ICE-CREAM GATEAU by first soaking the sponge with the soaking syrup and then topping with scoops of vanilla ice-cream and finely chopped pieces of mango.

44

Chocolate Nougat

A chocolate sponge topped with a creamy chocolate filling and coated with praline on the sides.

Preparation time : 15 to 20 minutes | **Cooking time : 35 minutes** | **Makes 4 to 6**

For the sponge cake

1 eggless chocolate cake, page 23, sliced into 2 horizontally

For the topping

200 grams chocolate, grated
200 grams fresh cream

For the nougat

1 recipe praline, page 102

To be mixed into a soaking syrup

½ cup water
2 tablespoons sugar

For the topping

1. Whip the cream till soft peaks form. Keep aside.
2. Melt the chocolate over a double boiler till it is smooth. Cool slightly.
3. Fold the cream into the warm chocolate and mix well. Keep aside.

How to proceed

1. Soak one layer of sponge with the soaking syrup. The other layer is not needed.
2. Wrap a 75 mm. (3") strip of greaseproof paper around the edge of the soaked sponge.
3. Pour the topping mixture onto this lined sponge.
4. Refrigerate for 2 to 3 hours till the topping has set.
5. Peel off the greaseproof paper strip carefully.
6. Coat the sides with praline.

Serve chilled.

Handy Tip

~ If you do not want to make praline, you can buy chikki and crush it.

Cherry Cream Flans   Picture on page 71

Individual flans topped with a cherry filling and fresh cream, garnished with flaked almonds.

Preparation time: 15 minutes	Cooking time: 5 minutes	Baking time: 15 to 20 minutes	Makes 5 flans

For the flans

1 recipe eggless sponge cake, page 22

For the cherry filling

2 cups whipped cream, page 106

1 small can cherries

3 teaspoons cornflour

2 teaspoons sugar

2 teaspoons lemon juice

a few drops cochineal (red) colour

1 to 2 drops almond essence

To be mixed into a soaking syrup

¾ cup water

2 tablespoons sugar

For the garnish

flaked almonds

For the flans

1. Spoon the cakemix into 5 small flan tins and bake in a hot oven at 200°C (400°F) for 15 to 20 minutes.

2. Remove from the tins and cool.

For the cherry filling

1. Stone the cherries. Keep aside the syrup.

2. To the fruit syrup, add the cornflour and sugar.

3. Boil for a little time. Stir till it becomes thick. Then add the cherries, lemon juice, colour and essence.

Handy Tip

~ You can make 1 big flan instead of 5 small ones.

How to proceed

1. Soak the flans with the sugar syrup.

2. Pipe whipped cream around the edge of the flans to make a border.

3. Spoon the filling mixture inside the cream border.

Garnish with flaked almonds.

Serve cold.

Tarts

My experience with tarts is that they are extremely easy to bake, and can be served as a snack as well as a dessert. They are mostly filled with seasonal or available fruit, jam, marmalade, chocolate and even cheese. A must at all English 'high teas' along with muffins, the tart made its way to India with the British army and has remained popular at many hill-stations all over the country, where it is sold from quaint old world bakeries with very English sounding names. It has recently sprung to rebirth in many 5 star hotels and speciality cake-shops in India's major cities.

Tarts

Preparation time: 15 min.   **Baking time: 15 min.**   **Makes 15 tartlets or one 200 mm. (8") diameter tart.**

200 grams plain flour (maida)

100 grams butter

1 tablespoon powdered sugar

a pinch of salt

1. Sieve the flour and salt together.

2. Rub the butter into the flour with the fingertips. Add the sugar and mix well.

3. Gradually add enough ice-cold water (approx. 2 to 3 tablespoons) to make a dough. Refrigerate for 10 to 15 minutes.

4. Lightly flour the rolling pin and the pastry board.

5. Roll out the pastry into a 6 mm. (¼") thickness.

6. Press it into a 200 mm. (8") diameter pie dish for making tarts.

7. To make smaller tarts, cut rounds of pastry using a large fluted cutter & press into patty tins (which need not be greased unless new).

8. Prick all over with a fork.

9. Bake blind in a hot oven at 230ºC (450ºF) for 10 to 15 minutes.

10. Cool the tart cases.

Lining a tart mould

Handy Tips

~ Use chilled butter as it gives a more crumbly pastry.

~ This dough can be made ahead of time and refrigerated, wrapped in plastic film.

Tart Shell

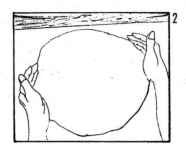
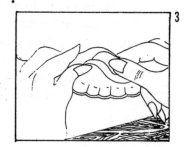

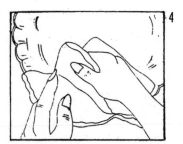
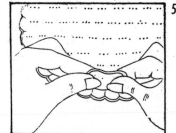
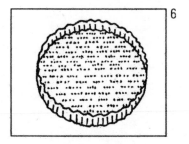

Strawberry And Pistachio Tartlets

A visually attractive delicious tea time snack of dainty pastry tartlets filled with slices of fresh strawberries, honey and cream and garnished with pistachios.

Preparation time : 20 minutes   Baking time : 20 minutes   Makes 15 tartlets.

For the tarts, page 50

For the filling

2 cups fresh strawberries, hulled and sliced

6 tablespoons honey

½ teacup whipped cream, page 106

¼ teaspoon vanilla essence

For the garnish

4 tablespoons pistachios, chopped

For the tarts

1. Remove the tart shells from the oven when they are lightly browned. Cool.

2. Invert the patty tins and gently tap the bottom to remove the shells.

For the filling

1. In a bowl, chop ½ cup of strawberries and mix with ¼ cup of whipped cream. Keep aside.

2. Mix the rest of the sliced strawberries with the honey and chill.

3. Whisk the remaining cream with the vanilla essence until soft. Keep aside.

How to proceed

1. Line the tartlets decoratively with sliced strawberries.

2. In the centre of each tartlet, put a spoonful of strawberries mixed with cream.

3. Pipe a swirl of whipped cream on the strawberries.

4. Sprinkle chopped pistachios on the whipped cream.

Serve chilled.

Handy Tips

~ Serve the tartlets in dainty paper cups.

~ When strawberries are not in season, use fresh mangoes.

Almond And Marmalade Tart

Slices of apple coated with marmalade baked to perfection in an almond pastry.

| Preparation time : **20** minutes | Baking time : **30** minutes | Makes 1 tart |

For the tart dough
200 grams plain flour (maida)
100 grams butter
1 tablespoon powdered sugar
100 grams ground almonds
a pinch salt

For the filling
350 grams cooking apples
juice of ½ lemon
2 tablespoons sugar
6 tablespoons marmalade

Other ingredients
1 tablespoon biscuit crumbs

For the tart dough

1. Rub the butter into the flour and salt with your finger tips. Add the sugar and almonds and mix well.

2. Gradually add enough ice-cold water (2 to 3 tablespoons) to make a dough. Refrigerate for 15 minutes.

For the filling

1. Peel and core the apples. Slice thinly into a bowl and sprinkle with the lemon juice.

2. Add the sugar and marmalade.

How to proceed

1. Preheat the oven to 200ºC (400ºF).

2. Roll out ¾ of the dough to 3 mm. (1/8") thickness and line a 200 mm. (8") diameter pie dish.

Lattice Work

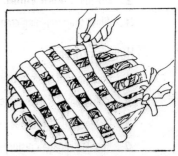

Grasshopper Pie, page 68.

52

3. Prick the pastry and sprinkle biscuit crumbs over it.

4. Spread the apple filling over it.

5. Roll out the left over dough into a thin sheet and cut into strips.

6. Cover with lattice strips (criss cross) of pastry.

7. Bake for 30 minutes till golden in colour.

8. Remove and cut into slices.

Serve hot or cold with cream or custard.

Blushing Cheese Tarts

A cold dessert of vanilla flavoured cheesecake in tartlets topped with a strawberry sauce.

Preparation time: 15 minutes   Baking time: 15 minutes   Cooking time: 15 to 20 minutes   Makes 15 tarts

For the tarts, page 50

For the filling

1 recipe cream cheese, page 108

¾ cup thick curds

4 to 5 tablespoons sugar

½ teaspoon vanilla essence

For the topping

strawberry sauce, page 105

For the filling

1. In a blender, liquidize the cream cheese, curds and sugar.

2. Taste and add extra sugar if required. Add the vanilla essence.

How to proceed

1. Fill each tart with a little filling. Refrigerate till the filling is firm.

2. Top with strawberry sauce.

Serve chilled.

Handy Tip

~ These need to be set for a few hours before you can pour the sauce over.

Variation

~ To make DAINTY CHERRY / PEACH CHEESECAKE, use cherry sauce or peach sauce, (page 103) instead of strawberry sauce.

◄   **Almond Strawberry Shortcake, page 56.**

Almond Strawberry Shortcakes Picture on page 54

Almond pastry biscuits sandwiched with strawberries and cream,
served with strawberry sauce.

Preparation time : 45 minutes	Baking time : 20 minutes	Makes 8 shortcakes

For the pastry

200 grams plain flour (maida)

100 grams butter

30 grams ground almonds

2/3 cup icing sugar

a pinch of salt

2 to 3 tablespoons ice-cold water

For the strawberry sauce

2 cups strawberries, hulled

2 tablespoons icing sugar

juice of ½ lemon

For the filling

1½ cups strawberries, sliced

1½ cups whipped cream, page 106

For the garnish

icing sugar to sprinkle

a few strawberries

For the pastry

1. Sieve the flour and salt together. Mix with the ground almonds.
2. Rub the butter into the flour with your fingertips. Add the sugar and mix well.
3. Add enough ice-cold water to make a dough. Chill for 30 minutes.
4. Preheat the oven to 200ºC (400ºF).
5. Roll out the pastry on a lightly floured surface and using a 100 mm. (4")

Handy Tips

~ You can also make these bite sized, if you use a smaller cookie cutter to cut the shortcake dough.

~ The dough can be refrigerated for a few days, wrapped in a plastic film.

fluted pastry cutter, cut sixteen rounds of 3 mm. (1/8") thickness.

6. Bake for 15 to 20 minutes until pale golden. Cool and keep aside the shortcakes.

For the strawberry sauce

1. Purée the strawberries in a blender. Add the icing sugar and lemon juice.

2. Strain and refrigerate.

How to proceed

1. Place one shortcake on a plate. Pipe some whipped cream on top and place some sliced strawberries thereon. Sandwich with another shortcake.

2. Make the other 7 shortcakes in the same manner.

For the garnish

Dust icing sugar on the top of each shortcake and garnish with strawberries.

Serve surrounded by the sauce.

Fruity Chocolate Tarts

Pastry tartlets lined with dark chocolate, filled with custard and slices of fresh fruit.

Preparation time : 10 minutes	Baking time : 15 minutes	Makes 15 tarts

For the tarts, page 50

For the chocolate base

½ cup dark chocolate, melted

For the custard

1½ cups milk

7 teaspoons sugar

2 tablespoons custard powder

½ teaspoon vanilla essence

¾ cup whipped cream, page 106

For the fruit topping

1 cup sliced fruit (stewed apple, peaches etc.)

For the chocolate base

Spread the warm melted chocolate on the inside of the cooled tarts and refrigerate.

For the custard.

1. Dissolve the custard powder in ½ cup of cold milk.
2. Heat the rest of the milk with the sugar.
3. When it boils, add the custard powder.
4. Cook for 1 minute and cool.
5. When cooled, gently fold in the whipped cream and the vanilla essence.

How to proceed

1. Pipe the custard on the chocolate lined tarts.
2. Top with sliced fruits of your choice.

Serve chilled.

Handy Tip

~ Use a pastry brush to spread the warm chocolate over the tarts.

Elegant Pies

$\mathcal{C}$lose your eyes and transport yourself to a country house in the scenic
English countryside. Summer is on and the flowers are in full bloom. You are at
a typical English tea-party. A wrought iron table in the far corner is laden with
all kinds of teatime goodies. Mysteriously, your hostess appears from within
holding before her a dish she has just cooked. "Come, sit down" she says,
"We were expecting you".....

Pies, have been popular all over Europe for centuries. Traditionally baked in a
pastry base with a variety of fillings, I have successfully altered the basic recipe
to suit our eggless concept of cooking.

Applejacks

The truly American oatmeal flapjack topped with apricot jam, cinnamon and sliced apples.

Preparation time : 15 minutes	Baking time : 30 to 35 minutes	Makes 12 pieces

For the crust

100 grams butter

100 grams brown sugar

120 grams rolled quick cooking oats

For the topping

3 tablespoons apricot jam

2 apples

1 tablespoon butter

½ teaspoon ground cinnamon

For the crust

1. Beat the butter and sugar very well until light and creamy.

2. Add the oats and mix well.

3. Press the mixture evenly into a greased shallow 175 mm. (7") square tin.

How to proceed

1. Melt the jam on a low flame. Spread about half the jam over the oat base in the pan.

2. Peel, core and thinly slice the apples. Arrange the apple slices on the top of the crust in three separate rows lengthwise, slightly overlapping the slices.

3. Add the butter and cinnamon to the remaining jam glaze and heat until the butter has melted. Brush this glaze over the apple slices.

4. Bake in a hot oven at 200°C (400°F) for 30 to 35 minutes or until the apples are tender and the flapjack base is golden brown.

5. Cut into pieces and let cool in the pan.

Serving Suggestion

~ Serve with vanilla ice-cream.

Chocolate Chiffon Pie

Chocolate mousse set in a crusty coconut base garnished with whipped cream and melted chocolate.

Preparation time: 15 minutes   **Cooking time: 15 minutes**   **Setting time: 1 to 2 hours**   **Serves 4 to 6**

For the coconut crust

1 cup grated coconut

2 tablespoons butter

2 tablespoons sugar

For the eggless mousse

1¼ cups milk

5 teaspoons sugar

1½ teaspoons cocoa powder

50 grams dark chocolate

5 grams agar agar (China grass), cut into small pieces

1 teaspoon custard powder

100 grams fresh cream

½ teaspoon vanilla essence

1 tablespoon powdered sugar

For the garnish

½ cup whipped cream, page 106

¼ cup melted chocolate

For the coconut crust

1. Heat the coconut in a flat bottom pan on a slow flame and stir continuously till it turns evenly brown. Cool.

2. Generously butter the bottom and sides of 175 mm. (7") diameter pie plate.

3. Mix the coconut, sugar and melted butter well.

4. Sprinkle the coconut mixture on the greased pie plate and press.

5. Chill until set.

For the eggless mousse

1. Soak the agar agar in ¾ cup of cold water for 1 hour. Heat on a slow flame until it dissolves.

2. Put 1 cup of milk to boil with the sugar, cocoa powder and dark chocolate.

3. To the balance ¼ cup milk, add the custard powder and boil. When the milk starts boiling, add to the cocoa mixture and continue stirring for 1 minute.

4. When the agar agar is dissolved completely, add to the boiling custard and cook again for 2 minutes.

5. Strain the mixture and continue stirring until it is slightly cool.

6. Beat the cream with the powdered sugar, add the vanilla essence and mix well. Add to the cocoa mixture and mix well.

How to proceed

1. Pour the mousse mixture into the coconut crust. Chill until firm.

2. Top with the whipped cream and drizzle with melted chocolate.

Cheesy Peach Pie

A delightful peach cheesecake on a crusty biscuit base.

| Preparation time: 15 minutes | Cooking time: 10 minutes | Setting time: 1 hour | Serves 6 |

For the crust

7 tablespoons crushed Marie biscuits

4 tablespoons melted butter

1 tablespoon sugar

For the filling

1 recipe cream cheese, page 108

1 can (450 grams) peaches,.drained

¾ cup thick curds

¾ cup castor sugar

For the decoration

whipped cream, page 106

For the crust

1. Mix the biscuits, butter and sugar and press the mixture evenly into a 175 mm. to 200 mm. (7" to 8") diameter loose bottomed tin.

2. Chill until firm.

For the filling

1. In a blender, liquidize the cream cheese with the curds and sugar.

2. Chop half the peaches and add to the mixture. Leave aside the remaining half for decoration.

How to proceed

1. Spread the filling over the crust and put to set in the refrigerator. This will require approximately 45 minutes to 1 hour.

2. Decorate with the remaining peaches and cream.

Cut into slices and serve cold.

Handy Tip

~ Use a muslin cloth to drain the curds. This takes about 15-20 minutes.

Italian Coffee Mousse In Coconut Crust

A coffee mousse flavoured with honey, set in a crunchy coconut crust.

Preparation time: 10 minutes	Cooking time: 10 minutes	Setting time: 1 hour	Serves 6

For the filling

8 teaspoons agar agar (China grass), cut into pieces

2 teaspoons instant coffee

2 teaspoons sugar

2 teaspoons honey

200 grams whipped cream, page 106

For the coconut crust

6 tablespoons grated fresh coconut

1 tablespoon butter

1 tablespoon brown sugar

To be mixed into a garnish

2 tablespoons desiccated coconut

1 teaspoon coffee powder

For the filling

1. Soak the agar agar in 250 ml. of cold water for 1 hour. Cook on a slow flame until it dissolves.

2. Add the coffee and the sugar. Strain the mixture.

3. Add the honey, mix well and allow to cool.

4. When the coffee mixture becomes syrupy and slightly thicker, add the whipped cream and mix well.

For the coconut crust

1. Mix the coconut, butter and brown sugar and cook on a slow flame for 2 minutes or until the coconut is slightly brown.

2. Spread this mixture on a greased 175 mm. (7") diameter glass dish.

3. Chill till firm.

How to proceed

Pour the filling mix on to the set coconut crust and refrigerate till set.

Serve chilled, garnished with the desiccated coconut flavoured with coffee powder.

Handy Tip

~ When cooking the coconut crust, it is important to keep stirring the mixture so it browns evenly.

Chocolate Devil Pie

A velvety chocolate and cream filling on a crunchy biscuit crust. A chocoholic's delight.

Preparation time : 15 minutes   **Setting time : 1 hour**   **Serves 6 to 8**

For the crust
200 grams crumbled chocolate or Bourbon biscuits
6 tablespoons butter
3 tablespoons powdered sugar

For the filling
200 grams milk chocolate, grated
1 cup whipped cream, page 106

For the garnish
whipped cream, page 106
grated chocolate

For the crust
1. Melt the butter, stir in the sugar and biscuit crumbs. Press the mixture with the back of a spoon on the sides and bottom of a shallow pie plate of 225 mm. (9") diameter to form the biscuit crust. {approx. 5 mm. (1/5") thick}

2. Chill till firm.

For the filling
1. Melt the chocolate in a little water over low heat. Do not boil.

2. Remove from the heat and allow to cool.

3. Stir in the whipped cream.

How to proceed
1. Spoon the chocolate mixture into the crust.

2. Chill till firm.

Serve with whipped cream and grated chocolate sprinkled on top.

Handy Tip

~ You could microwave the chocolate for a few seconds to melt it.

Mango Cheese Pie

A mango flavoured cheesecake on a ginger and walnut flavoured biscuit crust.

Preparation time: 20 minutes   Cooking time: 10 to 15 minutes   Setting time: 3 to 4 hrs.   Serves 4 to 6

For the crust

1 cup biscuit crumbs

1/3 cup broken walnut pieces

½ cup unsalted butter

a pinch dry ginger powder (soonth)

For the filling

2 mangoes, puréed

4 tablespoons thick curds

1 recipe cream cheese, page 108

¾ cup castor sugar

½ cup fresh cream

For the decoration

a few mango slices

a few walnut halves

For the crust

1. Grease a 200 mm. (8") loose bottomed tin (i.e. a kind of tin in which the sides of the tin be removed without disturbing or upturning the dessert).
2. Mix the biscuit crumbs, walnut pieces , butter and ginger powder very well.
3. Press evenly in the cake tin.
4. Chill until firm.

For the filling

1. In a blender, liquidise the mangoes, curds, cream cheese and sugar to a thick purée.
2. Whip the cream till soft peaks form and mix gently with the above mixture.

Handy Tip

~ Taste the mangoes for sweetness and adjust the sugar accordingly.

How to proceed

1. Pour the filling mixture on the set crust and refrigerate till set.

2. When set, unmould carefully.

Garnish with mango slices and walnut halves.

Serve chilled.

Grasshopper Pie   Picture on page 53

A delicate mint flavoured mousse set on a chocolate biscuit crust garnished with whipped cream and grated chocolate.

Preparation time: 15 minutes	Cooking time: 10 minutes	Setting time: 2 hours	Serves 4 to 6

For the crust

200 grams Bourbon biscuits, crushed
2 tablespoons melted butter

For the filling

2 cups milk
7 grams agar agar (China grass)
6 tablespoons sugar
1 cup whipped cream, page 106
¼ teaspoon green food colour
½ teaspoon mint essence

For the garnish

whipped cream, page 106
dark chocolate, grated

For the crust

1. Mix the crushed biscuits with the butter and line the bottom of a 175 mm. (7") loose bottomed pie tin.

2. Chill till set.

For the filling

1. Soak the agar agar in 1 cup of cold water for 1 hour. Cook on a slow flame until it dissolves.

2. Heat the milk and add the sugar and dissolved agar agar. Stir till it dissolves.

3. Strain the mixture and cool.

4. Fold in the whipped cream, add the colour and essence.

How to proceed

1. Pour the filling mixture over the set crust.

2. Refrigerate till the filling sets.

Garnish with whipped cream and grated chocolate.

Handy Tip

~ Use sprigs of mint and grated chocolate as an alternate garnish.

Quick Lemon Cheese Pie

Freshly whipped cream blended with lemon and cottage cheese chilled on a crunchy biscuit base.

| Preparation time: 10 minutes | Cooking time: 5 minutes | Setting time: 1 hour | Serves 4 to 5 |

For the Marie base

1 cup crumbled Marie biscuits

1/3 cup melted butter

For the filling

2/3 cup whipped cream, page 106

juice of 1½ lemons

grated rind of 1 lemon

1 cup cream cheese, page 108

½ cup powdered sugar

½ teaspoon lemon essence

For the garnish

½ cup biscuit crumbs

lemon wedges

For the base

1. Mix the biscuit crumbs with the melted butter and press the mixture into the base of a 175 mm. (7") diameter flan ring.

2. Chill until firm.

For the filling

Fold in the whipped cream with the lemon rind, juice, cream cheese, sugar and lemon essence.

How to proceed

Spread the filling over the base and chill until firm.

For the garnish

Remove the flan ring. Top the cheese pie with the biscuit crumbs forming criss cross patterns and decorate with lemon wedges.

Serve chilled.

Handy Tip

~ The best way to crumble biscuits is to put them in a plastic bag or a tea towel and crush using both hands till you get medium sized crumbs.

Serving Suggestion

~ Strawberry sauce complements this dessert very well.

Top to Bottom : Cherry Cream Flans, page 46;
Chocolate Peach Crêpes, page 79.

Pancakes

The beauty about a pancake is that it can be combined with a variety of fillings. Besides the basic pancake recipe, this section contains a selection of delicious fillings. Try them out for starters and you will grow in confidence. Later you can certainly innovate beyond the recipes featured here. Newer ideas will automatically strike you as you move along.

◄ Left to Right : Strawberry Sponge Roll, page 32;
Peach Fool with Fruits, page 88;
Tropical Fruit Salad with Coconut Cream Sauce, page 90.

Pancakes

½ cup plain flour (maida)

½ cup cornflour

3/4 cup milk

2 teaspoons melted butter

a pinch of salt

1. Mix the plain flour, cornflour, milk, salt and ½ cup of water. Mix very well until no lumps remain.

2. Grease a 125 mm. (5") diameter non-stick pan with the butter.

3. Pour 2 tablespoons of the batter, tilt the pan around quickly so that the batter coats the pan evenly.

4. When the sides starts to peel off, turn the pancake around and cook the other side for 30 seconds.

5. Repeat for the remaining batter, greasing the pan with butter when required:

Handy Tip

~ Pancakes can be made ahead of time and stored in plastic film.

Apple Crêpes

Delicious wafer thin crêpes folded over a spicy sweet apple filling and glazed with orange marmalade.

Preparation time : 10 minutes	Cooking time : 35 minutes	Makes 12 pancakes

For the pancakes, page 74

For the apple filling

4 apples, peeled and thickly sliced

2 tablespoons butter

4 tablespoons sugar

½ teaspoon cinnamon powder

Other ingredients

1 cup whipped cream, page 106

For the glaze

5 tablespoons orange marmalade

2 to 3 tablespoons water

a few drops of lemon juice

For the apple filling

1. Melt the butter.

2. Add the apple slices, sugar, cinnamon powder and continue cooking until the sugar has dissolved and the apple slices are well coated and soft. Cool and keep aside.

For the glaze

Mix all the ingredients in a pan and stir over gentle heat. Keep aside.

How to proceed

1. Spoon some of the apple filling carefully over each pancake and top with some of the whipped cream.

2. Roll the pancakes and place them in a pan containing the warm glaze.

Turn over and serve warm.

Handy Tip

~ Do not overcook the apples as the filling will become soggy, making it difficult to serve the crêpes.

Crêpes Georgette

A pineapple and strawberry combination interlaced between pancakes topped with powdered sugar and grilled till crusty.

Preparation time: 10 minutes	Baking time: 10 minutes	Cooking time: 20 minutes	Serves 4

For the pancakes, page 74

For the filling

6 pineapple slices, chopped

4 tablespoons sliced strawberries

2 tablespoons brown sugar

2 tablespoons butter

Other ingredients

melted butter for brushing

1 tablespoon powdered sugar

For serving

whipped cream, page 106

custard sauce, page 107

For the pancakes

1. Make the batter as specified in the basic recipe.

2. Make 4 large pancakes of about 150 mm. (6") diameter.

3. Keep aside.

For the filling

Heat the butter, add the brown sugar, pineapple and strawberries and cook for a while.

How to proceed

1. Place one pancake on a greased ovenproof dish, cover with a little of the filling mixture and another pancake.

2. Continue to stack the remaining pancakes with all the filling ending with a pancake on top.

Handy Tips

~ You can use any seasonal fruits in case strawberries are out of season.

~ To make CRÊPES GEORGETTE FLAMBÉ warm 4 tablespoons of brandy in a big spoon, set alight and pour over the pancakes.
Peaches can also be used instead of pineapple.

3. Brush with the melted butter and sprinkle the powdered sugar on top.
4. Bake in a hot oven at 200°C (400°F) for 10 minutes till golden in colour.
5. Cut into wedges and serve warm with whipped cream or custard sauce.

Caramel Banana Crêpes

Triangular pancakes of sweetened banana, flambéed with rum and served with whipped cream.

Preparation time : 10 minutes	Cooking time : 30 minutes	Makes 12 pancakes

For the pancakes, page 74

For the filling

4 ripe bananas, peeled and sliced

3 tablespoons brown sugar

3 tablespoons butter

For the flambé

2 tablespoons rum (optional)

To serve

whipped cream, page 106

For the filling

1. Melt the butter with the sugar in a pan.
2. Add the bananas and cook for about 2 to 3 minutes.

How to proceed

1. Fill the pancakes with the banana mixture and fold each pancake into a triangle.
2. To flambé the pancakes, lightly warm the rum in a big spoon, set alight and pour over the pancakes.

Serve with whipped cream.

Handy Tip

~ Rum greatly enhances the flavour of the bananas.

Variation

~ To make CARAMEL PEAR CRÊPES, use soft ripe pears instead of bananas. Prepare the pancakes and keep warm.

Hot Fudge Sundae Crêpes

A hot-cold dessert of crêpes rolled and filled with vanilla ice-cream and topped with a hot chocolate sauce and chopped nuts.

Preparation time : 10 minutes	Cooking time : 30 minutes	Makes 12 pancakes

For the pancakes, page 74

For the filling
12 scoops vanilla ice-cream

chocolate sauce, page

For the topping
whipped cream, page 106

roasted almonds

chopped walnuts

1. Fill each pancake evenly with 1 scoop of vanilla ice-cream and roll into cylindrical shape.
2. Warm the chocolate sauce in a pan.
3. Gently toss the stuffed pancakes in warm chocolate sauce and place on a plate.
4. Top with whipped cream, roasted almonds and chopped walnuts.

Handy Tips

~ You can use any flavour of ice-cream with the fudge sauce.

~ The ice-cream has to be very well frozen so that it does not melt quickly when the warm fudge sauce is poured over it.

Crêpes Belle Helene

Pancakes stuffed with stewed pears and topped with a rich chocolate sauce.

Preparation time : 10 minutes	Cooking time : 20 minutes	Makes 12 pancakes

For the pancakes, page 74

For the pear filling

4 medium sized pears, peeled and diced

4 tablespoons sugar

1 teaspoon lemon juice

1 teaspoon grated lemon rind

For the chocolate sauce

100 grams chocolate, grated

2 tablespoons milk

For the topping

1 tablespoon chopped almonds

For the pear filling

1. Place the pears in a saucepan and cover with ½ cup of water.

2. Add the sugar, lemon juice and rind and simmer gently until tender.

For the chocolate sauce

1. Melt the chocolate in a bowl over a pan of hot water, stirring continuously. Add milk to make a sauce-like consistency.

2. Keep aside.

How to proceed

1. Fill each pancake with a portion of the pear filling.

2. Fold and top with some chocolate sauce and sprinkle with chopped almonds.

Variation

~ CHOCOLATE PEACH CRÊPES : (Picture on page 71) You can use peaches instead of pears and trickle some of the fudge sauce over the pancakes.

Caribbean Crêpes

From the land of the 'pina colada', a sweetened coconut and pineapple filling rolled into pancakes and topped with a warm custard sauce.

Preparation time : 15 minutes	Cooking time : 35 minutes	Makes 12 pancakes

For the pancakes, page 74

For the custard sauce, page 107

For the filling

1 small can (450 grams) pineapple slices, finely chopped

6 tablespoons grated coconut

2 tablespoons sugar

2 tablespoons butter

For the filling

1. Heat the butter and the sugar in a pan and toss in the pineapples and coconut.

2. Stir till the sugar dissolves and keep aside.

How to proceed

1. Fill the pancakes with the filling and roll them into cylindrical shape.

2. In a pan, heat the custard sauce and gently toss in the rolled pancakes.

3. Turn over, cook for half a minute and serve warm.

Handy Tip

~ You can serve these with coconut cream sauce, (page 90) or plain custard sauce, (page 107)

Quick Fix-ups

As the name suggests, if your mother-in-law drops by all of a sudden, wouldn't your heart miss a beat!? Guests always possess that uncanny knack of showing up at your doorstep when you least expect them. Now all you'll have to do is to hurry to your kitchen shelf and very discreetly refer to any of the recipes in this section. All ingredients are the ones normally in stock in the house or easily available at the nearby grocer. Many a time, I have saved myself from an embarrassing situation. If you can read between the lines of my recipes in this section, you'd probably laugh along with me all the way to the kitchen.

Ice-Cream Pie On A Coconut Crust

Savour the deliciously contrasting textures of soft ice-cream on a crisply roasted coconut base.

Preparation time : 10 minutes	Setting time : 30 minutes	Serves 6 to 8

For the coconut crust

2 cups desiccated coconut

4 tablespoons butter

2 tablespoons sugar

For the filling

4 cups ice-cream (combination of vanilla, strawberry, chocolate)

To serve

strawberry sauce, page 105

For the coconut crust

1. Roast the coconut in a broad pan. Cool.
2. Add the melted butter and sugar. Mix well.
3. Generously butter the bottom and sides of a 225 mm. (9") diameter pie plate.
4. Sprinkle the coconut mixture and press it down with your palm.
5. Chill until set.

How to proceed

1. Top the coconut crust with scoops of ice-cream and spread it evenly.
2. Serve with strawberry sauce.

Handy Tips

~ To make small individual pies, line the crust mixture in 6 small bowls and set. Then top with scoops of ice-cream and serve with any sauce of your choice.

~ You can also use freshly grated coconut instead of dessicated coconut to make the crust juicier.

Fruit Brochettes   Picture on page 17

Well marinated seasonal fruit skewered and grilled in the oven, then flambéed with rum makes a very colourful low calorie dessert.

Preparation time : 15 minutes	Grilling time : 5 minutes	Makes 8 skewers

3 cups fresh or canned fruits (strawberries, peaches, bananas, pineapples, black grapes) cut into big pieces

For the marinade
grated rind and juice of 1 lemon
2 tablespoons honey

For the flambé
2 tablespoons rum or brandy (optional)

1. Place all the fruits in a shallow dish.

2. In a small bowl, mix together the lemon juice, rind and honey.

3. Pour this mixture over the fruits and leave to marinate for 10 to 15 minutes.

4. Lift the fruits out of the marinade and arrange different fruits alternately onto 8 small thin skewers.

5. Place the skewers in an ovenproof baking dish and grill in a preheated oven at 200°C (400°F) for 2 to 3 minutes.

6. Warm the rum in a big spoon, set alight and pour over the skewers.

Serve at once.

Handy Tips

~ Arrange contrasting colored fruits next to each other so that the brochettes look visually appealing.

~ You can also use tooth picks instead of skewers.

Crunchy Peach Custard

A warm delicious dessert of stewed peaches topped with custard and crunchy caramelised sugar.

Preparation time: 5 minutes	Cooking time: 5 to 10 minutes	Baking time: 15 minutes	Serves 6

3 tablespoons custard powder

2 tablespoons sugar

2 cups milk

1 small can (450 grams) peaches

2 tablespoons brown sugar

1. Mix the custard powder and the sugar with a little milk to form a smooth cream.
2. Heat the rest of the milk. Pour onto the mixed custard powder, stirring well.
3. Bring to the boil stirring continuously for 2 minutes.
4. Drain the peaches and arrange the peach halves in an ovenproof dish.
5. Pour the hot custard over the inverted peach halves.
6. Sprinkle the brown sugar on top and bake in a hot oven at 200°C (400°F) for 15 minutes.

Serve warm when the sugar topping is crisp.

Handy Tips

~ Always keep stirring the custard while cooking as it tends to stick to the vessel or form lumps.

~ You can use stewed apples or pears instead of peaches.

Miami Cup

Layers of chocolate ice-cream, whipped cream and orange sauce, topped with crunchy roasted coconut served in ice-cream glasses.

Preparation time : 5 minutes   **Cooking time : 5 minutes**   **Makes 6 glasses**

6 scoops chocolate ice-cream

1 teacup orange sauce, page 103

1 cup fresh cream

3 tablespoons powdered sugar

2 tablespoons fresh coconut, grated

1. Whisk the cream with the sugar until thick.

2. Roast the coconut in a pan.

3. Arrange the ice-cream, whipped cream and orange sauce in layers in six individual glasses.

4. Top with the roasted coconut.

Serve immediately.

Handy Tip

~ You could use any other flavour of ice-cream.

Chocolate Truffles

Easy to make rum and coffee flavoured chocolate truffles rolled in castor sugar, cocoa powder and walnuts.

Preparation time : 15 minutes	Cooking time : 5 minutes	Makes 30 truffles

250 grams chocolate, grated

½ cup unsalted butter

1 cup icing sugar

1 teaspoon coffee

2 tablespoons rum (optional)

For the garnish

castor sugar and cocoa powder

2 tablespoons walnuts, chopped

1. Mix the coffee with 2 tablespoons of hot water.
2. Melt the chocolate and butter in a pan. Add the sugar and coffee liquid.
3. Beat lightly. Add rum if desired and remove from the fire.
4. Cool and refrigerate till firm.
5. Roll into small balls and keep-aside.

For the garnish

1. Mix the cocoa powder, castor sugar and chopped walnuts in a plate.
2. Roll the truffle balls in this mixture.

Serve in small paper cups.

Handy Tips

~ Cook the chocolate on very low heat as it tends to burn very quickly leaving an unpleasant taste.

~ If refrigerated, these could be stored up to a fortnight.

Drunken Grapes

A chilled brandy flavoured dessert of grapes topped with fresh cream and melted sugar.

Preparation time : 5 minutes	Grilling time : 10 minutes	Serves 6

2 cups green seedless grapes

2 tablespoons brandy

200 grams whipped cream, page 106

6 tablespoons brown sugar

1. Slice the grapes.

2. Place them in a bowl, add the brandy and marinate for 5 minutes.

3. Put the grapes in a 150 mm. (6") diameter ovenproof dish.

4. Cover with the cream and sprinkle the brown sugar on top.

5. Place the dish under a very hot grill until the sugar melts.

6. Chill for 1 hour before serving.

Handy Tips

~ You can use any other fruit or liqueur.

~ Pre-heat the grill before you place the dish under it, as the cream could break down under fluctuating temperatures.

Mango Ice-Cream

Pieces of chilled King Alphonso puréed with sugar and cream and set in the freezer.

Preparation time : 20 minutes	Setting time : 4 to 6 hours	No cooking	Serves 6 to 8

6 large ripe Alphonso mangoes, peeled

8 tablespoons powdered sugar

500 grams cream, chilled

1. Cut half the mangoes into small cubes and purée the other half. Mix and keep aside.

2. Whip the cream and the sugar till thick.

3. Combine the mangoes (purée and chopped pieces) with the whipped cream.

4. Pour the mixture into an aluminium container and freeze.

Note : It is not necessary to beat this ice-cream again as the texture is smooth and velvety.

Handy Tips

~ All ingredients should be chilled before mixing so that they set together thus avoiding crystallization.

~ Ice-cream sets best and quickest in aluminium containers, covered with aluminium foil.

Peach Fool

Peaches, blended with custard and brandy topped with whipped cream and garnished with grated chocolate.

Preparation time: 10 minutes	Cooking time: 10 minutes	Setting time: 1 hour	Serves 6

For the peach mixture

1 small can (225 grams) peaches

3 teaspoons brandy (optional)

3 teaspoons lemon juice

1 teaspoon vanilla essence

2 tablespoons thick curds

3 tablespoons custard powder

500 ml. milk

2 tablespoons brown sugar

150 ml. whipped cream, page 106

For the decoration

extra whipped cream, page 106

grated plain chocolate

1. Drain the peaches and liquidise them with the brandy, lemon juice, vanilla essence and curds. Keep aside.

2. Mix the custard powder in ½ cup of cold milk. Boil the rest of the milk with the brown sugar. When the milk starts boiling, add the custard powder, cook for 1 minute and cool.

3. Mix the cooled custard with the peach mix.

4. Fold in the whipped cream into the peach mixture.

5. Pour into the individual dishes. Refrigerate till set.

6. When you wish to serve, decorate with extra whipped cream and grated chocolate and serve cold.

Handy Tip

~ You can also set this dessert in tall fluted glasses.

Variation

~ PEACH FOOL WITH FRUITS - Pour the peach mixture over fresh fruit pieces, put to set in tall glasses and serve chilled. (Picture on page 72)

Tembleque

A Latin American favourite of chilled coconut cream custard served with a combination of two fruit sauces flavoured with dark rum.

Preparation time: 10 minutes	Cooking time: 5 minutes	Setting time: 2 hours	Serves 4 to 6

For the coconut custard

3 cups coconut milk

½ cup sugar

½ cup cornflour

For the mango sauce

2 medium sized mangoes, puréed and strained

2 tablespoons dark rum (optional)

For the strawberry sauce

1 ½ cups strawberries, puréed and strained

½ cup sugar

2 tablespoons dark rum (optional)

For the mango sauce

Flavour the mango purée with rum and refrigerate overnight.

For the strawberry sauce

Add the sugar to the strawberry purée. Flavour with rum and refrigerate overnight.

For the coconut custard

1. Mix all the ingredients in a pan and heat, stirring constantly.

2. Stir till the mix is thick enough to coat the back of a spoon.

3. Cool and pour the custard into individual moulds.

How to proceed

1. Refrigerate for 2 hours or until set.

2. Unmould and serve with the two sauces.

Handy Tip

~ Use a non-stick pan to make the coconut custard and stir continuously.

Variation

~ Any fresh fruit sauce can be used if mango and strawberry are not in season.

Tropical Fruit Salad With Coconut Cream
Sauce Picture on page 72

A mixed tropical fruit cocktail of lychees, strawberries, watermelon, melon and mango served with a coconut cream sauce.

Preparation time : 10 minutes	Cooking time : 10 minutes	Serves 6

For the fruit salad

½ cup lychees, de-seeded
½ cup strawberries, halved
½ cup watermelon, diced
½ cup grapes, halved
½ cup melon balls
½ cup mangoes, diced

For the coconut cream sauce

1 cup coconut cream, page 105
4 teaspoons cornflour
5 tablespoons sugar
2 tablespoons fresh cream
¼ teaspoon rose essence

For the coconut cream sauce

1. Dissolve the cornflour in 1 cup of water.
2. Heat the coconut cream with the sugar and when it comes to a boil, add the cornflour mixed with water.
3. Simmer for 1 minute and strain.
4. Cool completely.
5. Add the fresh cream and flavour with the rose essence.
6. Refrigerate till chilled.

How to proceed

1. Arrange the fruits in 6 serving bowls.
2. Pour the coconut cream sauce on top of the fruit.

Serve chilled, garnished with mint leaves.

Handy Tip

~ You can use a melon scoop to get round balls of fruit.

Strawberry Soufflé   Picture on page 17

A low calorie recipe for the classic soufflé.

Preparation time : a few minutes	No cooking	Serves 4

1½ cups cream cheese, page 108

½ cup whipped cream, page 106

3 to 4 tablespoons strawberry crush or

10 to 12 fresh strawberries mashed with 2 tablespoons sugar

For the garnish

whipped cream, page 106

fresh strawberries

1. Mix the mashed strawberries with the cream cheese.

2. Gently fold in the whipped cream.

3. Adjust the sugar to your liking.

4. Pour into individual moulds and refrigerate till set.

Serve garnished with whipped cream and strawberries.

Handy Tip

~ You can use an equal quantity of any other fruit of your choice.

Warm & Cozy Desserts

Give me a cold rainy night and I'd serve you a hot soup and a hearty meal to end with a warm and cosy dessert. These could range from the simple Bread & Butter Pudding to the exotic Christmas Pudding which when set alight becomes the 'tour de force' of the evening.

Pineapple, Banana And Fig Flambé

Combination fruits, lightly baked in the oven, sprinkled with dark rum and set aflame.

Preparation time : a few minutes	Baking time : 20 to 25 minutes	Serves 6

10 firm bananas

1 medium sized pineapple

½ cup dried fig or 2 large fresh figs

2 tablespoons butter

½ cup brown sugar

3 tablespoons lemon juice

¼ teaspoon ground cardamom

¼ teaspoon ground cinnamon

2 tablespoons chopped almonds

4 tablespoons rum (optional)

1. Peel and thickly slice the bananas.

2. Core and cut the pineapple into 25 mm. (1") chunks.

3. Cut the dried figs into strips or peel and chop the fresh figs.

4. Place the bananas in a shallow ovenproof dish and top with the pineapple and fig pieces.

5. Melt the butter in a saucepan. Stir in the brown sugar, lemon juice, cardamom powder, cinnamon and heat until well mixed. Pour over the fruits.

6. Cover lightly and cook in a hot oven at 200°C (400°F) for 20 to 25 minutes.

7. Remove and sprinkle with almonds.

8. Heat the rum, ignite and pour over the fruit. Serve immediately.

Handy Tips

~ Always heat the liquor lightly before setting it alight.

~ Ice - cream is a good accompaniment to this dessert.

Chinese Toffee Apples

Deep-fried crispy apple fritters soaked in honey syrup and topped with sesame seeds.

Preparation time : 10 minutes	Cooking time : 20 minutes	Serves 4 to 6

4 ripe apples, peeled, cored, cut in wedges

For the batter

3 tablespoons plain flour (maida)

3 tablespoons cornflour

For the syrup

¼ cup oil

¼ cup sugar

¼ cup honey

2 tablespoons sesame seeds

Other ingredients

oil for deep frying

iced water to serve with fritters

Handy Tip

~ Prepare the syrup as close to serving time as possible. It only takes a few minutes and the results will be much better.

For the batter

1. Mix the flour and cornflour and sift in a bowl. Make the batter with 5 tablespoons of water and keep aside for 10 to 15 minutes.

2. Dip the apple wedges in this batter and deep fry till golden brown.

For the syrup

1. Keep aside all the fritters.

2. In another pan, heat the oil, add the sugar and heat, stirring constantly, until the sugar dissolves and caramelises lightly . Stir in the honey and the sesame seeds.

3. Keep warm.

How to proceed

1. Pierce each fritter with a tooth pick and place on a plate.

2. Pour the warm syrup in one bowl and pour ice-cold water in another bowl.

3. When ready to eat, dip each fritter in the warm syrup and then in ice-cold water. This will cause the syrup coating to harden so the fritters will be crisp and crackling on the outside surface.

Pineapple Supreme

Whole pineapple, baked with a flavoured stuffing.

Preparation time : 15 minutes	Cooking time : 1 hour	Serves 6

1 large pineapple

1 cup brown sugar

2 tablespoons rum (optional)

2 tablespoons butter

200 grams whipped cream, page 106

1. Slice off the pineapple top to make a 'lid'. Trim the base of the pineapple so that it stands upright.

2. Scoop out the flesh and cut into pieces, removing the core.

3. Sweeten with the sugar and flavour with the rum, then put the mixture back into the pineapple shell.

4. Dot the top with knobs of butter and wrap the pineapple in aluminium foil.

5. Wrap the 'lid' separately in foil.

6. Stand the pineapple upright on a baking sheet and bake in a hot oven at 200°C (400°F) for 1 hour.

7. Remove the foil and cover with the 'lid'.

8. Place the pineapple on a serving dish.

Serve with whipped cream in a separate bowl.

Handy Tip

~ Since a lot of juices will be released during baking, it is advisable to place the pineapple on a tray in the oven and not on a wire grill.

Assorted Fruit Fritters

Batter fried fruit wedges dusted with powdered sugar.

Preparation time : 10 minutes	Cooking time : 10 minutes	Serves 6 to 8

For the batter

3 teacups plain flour (maida)

1 tablespoon baking powder

a pinch of salt

1 teacup milk

For the fruits

1 to 2 firm mangoes, cut

3 to 4 firm bananas , cut

3 to 4 pineapple slices, cut

Other ingredients

¼ cup plain flour (maida)

¼ teaspoon cinnamon powder

oil for deep frying

For serving

powdered sugar to sprinkle

1. Prepare the batter by mixing the flour, baking powder and salt and sifting in a mixing bowl.
2. Mix the milk and 1½ cups of water and add gradually to the sifted flour mixture to make a smooth batter of coating consistency. Keep aside for 10 to 15 minutes.
3. Mix the plain flour and cinnamon powder and sprinkle over the fruit pieces.
4. Dip the fruit pieces in the batter, coat well and deep fry in hot oil till golden crisp. Drain.
5. Roll in powdered sugar and serve.

Handy Tip

~ You could serve a fruit sauce with these fritters.

Bread And Butter Pudding

A popular favourite at Mumbai's Irani Restaurants, a dessert of bread and milk baked with a topping of raisins and nuts.

Preparation time : 10 minutes	Baking time : 20 minutes	Serves 4 to 6

For the pudding

4 to 6 bread slices

1½ tablespoons butter

2 tablespoons cornflour

¾ cup sugar

2 cups milk

2 tablespoons walnuts

2 tablespoons raisins

½ teaspoon vanilla essence

For the topping

1 tablespoon brown sugar

2 tablespoons butter

¼ teaspoon ground nutmeg

1. Remove the crust from the bread slices, spread the butter on the slices and cut each slice into 2 to 3 strips.

2. Arrange the strips in a greased 200 mm. (8") diameter pie dish.

3. Combine the cornflour and sugar and make a paste with a little milk.

4. Boil the rest of the milk & stir in the paste after lowering the heat.

5. Add the vanilla essence and stir continuously until the sauce becomes thick and smooth. Remove and keep aside.

6. Sprinkle the raisins and walnuts on the bread and pour the sauce over it. Top with the brown sugar and knobs of butter.

7. Bake in a hot oven at 180°C (350°F) for 20 minutes.

8. Remove and sprinkle the nutmeg powder on top.
   Serve hot.

Handy Tip

~ Since the pudding is served in the same dish in which it is baked in, use a glass dish and not an aluminium baking dish.

Apple Strudel

A traditional Austrian classic of apples cooked with bread crumbs and raisins in a light paper – thin pastry.

Preparation time : 30 minutes   **Baking time : 45 minutes**   **Serves 4 to 6**

For the dough

1½ cups plain flour (maida)

1 tablespoon powdered sugar

½ teaspoon salt

2 tablespoons oil

For the filling

100 grams butter

1 cup fresh white bread crumbs

2 cups finely chopped apples

2 cups raisins

2 tablespoons currants

4 tablespoons sugar

½ teaspoon ground cinnamon

2 teaspoons finely grated lemon rind

2 tablespoons brown sugar

1 teaspoon lemon juice

For the decoration

icing sugar or powdered sugar

For the dough

1. Sieve together the flour, sugar and salt.
2. Make a well in the centre and add the oil.
3. Add warm water gradually, stirring with a fork to make a soft sticky dough.
4. Knead the dough.
5. Form into a ball, place in a bowl and cover with a warm cloth. Leave to rest for 1 hour.

For the filling

1. Melt half the butter in a pan and fry the bread crumbs until they are crisp and golden.

2. Add fhe remaining ingredients and cook for 3 to 4 minutes until the apples soften.

How to proceed

1. Using a rolling pin, roll out the dough into a rectangle as thinly as possible, lifting and turning it to prevent it from sticking. Using the back of your hands, gently stretch the dough, working from the.centre to the outside until it is paper thin - you should be able to read through the dough, but to do this takes years of practice and patience. Leave the dough to rest for 15 minutes.

2. Melt the remaining butter and use most of it to brush all over the dough. Spread the filling on the dough to within 25 mm. (1") of the edges.

3. Lift the two corners of the dough nearest to you and roll the dough away from you. Place the dough on a greased baking sheet and form into a horseshoe.

4. Brush all over with the remaining melted butter.

5. Bake in a preheated oven at 200ºC (400ºF) for 15 minutes, then lower the heat to 150ºC (300ºF) and bake for an additional 30 minutes.

Serve warm or cold, dusted with icing sugar and cut into slices.

Basic
Recipes

Praline Powder No. 1

Preparation time : 10 minutes	Cooking time : 10 minutes	Makes about 1 cup

¾ cup almonds or cashewnuts or peanuts or walnuts, roasted and chopped

¾ to 1 cup sugar

oil for greasing

1. Melt the sugar in a heavy saucepan and add the nuts.
2. Spread the mixture on an oiled surface, allow to cool and harden.
3. Powder coarsely and store in an air-tight jar.

Handy Tips

~ Use a wooden spoon to stir, as metal spoons conduct heat quickly.

~ As sugar caramelises quickly, make sure you pay attention during the heating process.

Praline Powder No. 2

Preparation time : a few minutes	Cooking time : 10 minutes	Makes ¾ cup

½ cup sugar

½ teaspoon vanilla essence

¾ teacup almonds, blanched and browned

oil for greasing

1. Put the sugar and vanilla in a heavy bottomed pan.
2. Melt over a medium heat until it is brown.
3. Add the almonds, mix well and pour onto an oiled surface. Cool and then pound as finely as possible.

Rabdi

Preparation time : 2 minutes	Cooking time : 10 to 15 minutes	Makes 1 cup

½ litre milk

50 grams sugar

1. Heat the milk in a broad pan and keep stirring on low heat till it is reduced to one-third.
2. Add the sugar and simmer till the milk becomes thicker.

Handy Tip

~ Use a non-stick pan as it prevents the milk from sticking and burning.

Orange Sauce

Preparation time : a few minutes **Cooking time : 3 to 5 minutes** **Makes 1 cup**

1 teacup orange juice

2 tablespoons orange squash

3 teaspoons sugar

2 level teaspoons cornflour

½ teaspoon orange colouring

a few drops orange essence

½ teaspoon lemon juice

1. Mix the orange juice, orange squash, sugar and cornflour and cook until thick. Allow to cool.

2. Add the colouring, essence and lemon juice.

Handy Tips

~ This sauce can be used to top vanilla ice-cream.

~ Do not cook the sauce in an aluminium or copper vessel, as it will turn black and have a rancid taste.

Cherry Sauce / Peach Sauce

Preparation time : a few minutes **Cooking time : a few minutes** **Makes 2 to 3 cups**

1 small can (450 grams) cherries or peaches

2 teaspoons cornflour

2 teaspoons sugar

2 teaspoons lemon juice

a few drops cochineal (for cherry sauce only)

1. Stone the cherries (or chop the peaches).

2. To the fruit syrup, add the cornflour and sugar.

3. Boil for a little time. Stir till it becomes thick. Then add the lemon juice and fruit (also cochineal colour in case of cherry sauce). Pour the hot mixture into a bowl. Cool and refrigerate.

Handy Tip

~ A quick and easy topping, ideal for unexpected guests.

Fudge Sauce

Preparation time : 5 minutes	Cooking time : 5 minutes	Makes 2½ cups

150 grams plain chocolate

1 teaspoon sugar

9 tablespoons boiling water

3 tablespoons butter

1 tablespoon golden syrup

2 teaspoons vanilla essence

1. Grate the chocolate.

2. Heat the sugar, water and butter and cook until the sugar has melted.

3. Add the golden syrup and the grated chocolate.

4. Cook until the chocolate melts completely.

5. Cool a little and then add the vanilla essence.

Handy Tips

~ If possible, use a double boiler.

~ Use gentle heat, as chocolate tends to burn quickly.

Orange Butter Sauce

Preparation time : a few minutes	Cooking time : 4 to 5 minutes	Makes 2 cups

2 cups orange juice

4 tablespoons powdered sugar

2 teaspoons cornflour

1 tablespoon butter

1. Melt the butter in a pan. Add the orange juice and sugar and bring it to one boil.

2. Mix the cornflour with a little water.

3. Pour the cornflour into the orange juice mixture.

4. Cook until the sauce thickness and coats the back of a spoon.

5. Cool and use as required.

Coconut Cream

Preparation time : 10 minutes	No cooking	Makes 2 cups

1 fresh coconut

1 cup boiling water

1. Grate the coconut. Pour boiling water over it and leave for 30 minutes.

2. Put it in muslin cloth and squeeze out.

3. This first pressing produces coconut cream, which after several hours of refrigeration acquires the density of double cream.

Handy Tip

~ Grate only the white part of the coconut avoiding the brown skin as it will change the colour of the cream.

Brandy Butter

Preparation time : 5 minutes	Cooking time : 5 to 7 minutes	Makes 1½ cups

½ cup unsalted butter

1 cup castor sugar

2 tablespoons brandy

1. Beat the butter and sugar until light and fluffy.

2. Pour a little brandy at a time and mix.

Strawberry Sauce

Preparation time : a few minutes	Cooking time : 3 to 5 minutes	Makes 1 cup

1 cup crushed strawberries

7 teaspoons sugar

2 level teaspoons cornflour

1 cup water

juice of ½ lemon

a few drops red colouring

Mix all the ingredients and cook for a few minutes.

Handy Tip

~ For a smoother sauce, strain to remove the seeds.

Whipped Cream

For decoration and serving.

Preparation time : a few minutes	No cooking	Makes 4 cups

400 grams cream

4 to 5 tablespoons powdered sugar

¼ teaspoon vanilla essence

1. Chill the cream for at least 2 hours as the cream has to be very cold for whipping.

2. Put it into a bowl and beat until it doubles in volume and forms soft peaks.

3. Carefully fold in the sugar and vanilla essence.

Serve with any dessert or use as a garnish.

Handy Tips

~ In hot weather, beat the cream over a platter of crushed ice.

~ Be careful not to overbeat this cream, as it can separate the butter from the cream, leaving it lumpy.

How To Make A Pastry Bag

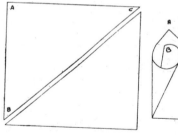
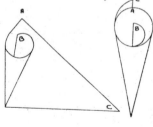

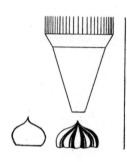
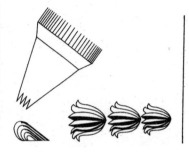
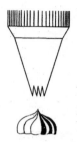

Custard Sauce

| Preparation time : 3 minutes | Cooking time : 5 minutes | Makes 2 cups |

2 cups milk

4 teaspoons sugar

2 level teaspoons custard powder

½ teaspoon vanilla essence

1. Mix the custard powder in ½ cup of cold milk to a smooth paste.

2. Put the rest of the milk to boil with the sugar.

3. When the milk starts boiling, add the custard mixture gradually.

4. Cook for 1 minute.

5. Cool the sauce and add the vanilla essence.

Handy Tips

~ Increase the quantity of custard powder to obtain a thick sauce.

~ It is important to keep stirring the sauce continuously, so that the custard does not get lumps or stick to the bottom of the pan.

~ Use a non-stick pan if available.

Apricot Sauce

| Preparation time : a few minutes | Cooking time : 5 minutes | Makes 2 cups |

250 grams dried apricots

4 tablespoons sugar

juice of 1 lemon

1. Wash the apricots and soak in just enough water to cover them.

2. After 4 hours, remove the seeds, add the sugar, bring to a boil and cook for 4 minutes.

3. Pass the mixture through a sieve.

4. Cool the sauce and add the lemon juice.

5. Chill.

Cream Cheese

Preparation time : a few minutes | **Cooking time : 10 minutes** | **Makes 1½ cups (approx.)**

1 litre full fat milk

1 teaspoon citric acid crystals

½ cup warm water

1. Put the milk to boil in a thick bottomed pan.
2. When it comes to a boil, remove from the flame and keep aside for a few minutes.
3. In another bowl, mix the citric acid crystals with the warm water.
4. Pour this mixture into the hot milk and allow to stand for about 5 minutes till the milk curdles on its own. Stir gently if required.
5. Strain this mixture using a muslin cloth.
6. Blend the drained milk solids in a food processor till smooth and creamy.

Use as required.

Handy Tip

~ If the drained whey is milky, boil it once more and strain the separated milk solids.

Paneer

Preparation time : a few minutes | **Cooking time : 10 minutes** | **Makes 1 cup**

1 litre full cream milk

2 teaspoons lemon juice

1. Put the milk to boil. When it starts boiling, switch off the gas and wait for a while.
2. Add the lemon juice and when the milk curdles, strain using a muslin cloth.

Use as required in the recipe.

Handy Tips

~ You can also use vinegar instead of lemon juice.

~ If you want solid paneer, put some weight on the drained paneer and leave it on for some time.